Lifeline

THE THIRD AGE is the period of life after full-time, gainful employment and family responsibility. Nowadays, it may last for thirty years or more and should be a time of fulfilment and continuing personal development … a time of regeneration.

The Third Age Press aims to provide inspiration for that regeneration. We hope that our publications will also give pleasure and lead the users into many rewarding pursuits.

Lifelines was the first series to be published by Third Age Press. It is specifically designed to stimulate reflection — to see the lines that connect your life not only to the past, but to the present and future as well. We hope it will encourage you to record, in some fashion, a picture of a unique individual.

Lifelines is dedicated to my mother, Victoria Lloyd, a woman of great character, creativity and originality, without whom, for many reasons, Third Age Press would never have existed.

Dianne Norton, Managing Editor

Third Age Press

ISBN 898576 00 9 First edition 1993

Second edition 2001

Re-printed 2005

Third Age Press, 6 Parkside Gardens, London SW19 5EY

www.thirdagepress.co.uk

Original design by Finlayson Design, London
Illustrated by Peter Ross
Printed in Great Britain by Rushmere Printers, London

Lifelines

A Voyage
of Rediscovery

A guide to writing your life story

by Eric Midwinter

Third Age Press

Professor Eric Midwinter, D Phil MA OBE,
lately Director of the Centre for Policy on Ageing, is a founder
member of the University of the Third Age, and a noted expert
on reminiscence and self-history.

He has over fifty books to his credit,
ranging over several fields.
They include:

Victorian Social Reform Education For Sale

Priority Education

Old Liverpool

Make'em Laugh: Famous Comedians and Their Worlds

W G Grace: His Life And Times

The Illustrated History of County Cricket

Age is Opportunity: Education and Older People

The Wage of Retirement

Yesterdays: The Way We Were, 1919 - 1939

Other publications in the *Lifelines* series

Encore: A Guide to Planning a Celebration of Your Life

*The Rhubarb People: Eric Midwinter's
'Voyage of Rediscovery'*

Getting to Know Me

Also for Third Age Press:

Best Remembered: a hundred stars of yesteryear

Novel Approaches: a guide to the popular classic novel

500 Beacons: the U3A story

A Voyage of Rediscovery

A guide to writing your life story

Why launch the boat?

Why bother? Why should you, an older person, either waste what might be valuable time on, or get involved in the shassle of, a voyage of rediscovery? For this suggested journey is not into the unknown; it is into the all too well-known. It is a voyage backwards into the oceanic turbulence of your own past, in an endeavour to prepare a history of yourself.

IT MIGHT DO YOU GOOD

There are several reasons which you might wish to consider. It is possible that reminiscence of this kind is therapeutic, in the sense of keeping the mind active and in touch with reality. Indeed, there is a clinical form of this activity, known as reminiscence-therapy which claims to be about, in certain cases, exactly that kind of reality orientation. In fact, the practice of 'Reality Orientation' is designed to stimulate people into re-learning basic facts about themselves and the world in which they live.

This booklet is not to be used, like the half-bottle of whisky hidden in the bottom drawer of the sideboard, 'purely for medicinal purposes'.

Its aim is much wider than that. However, the sheer value of mental alertness being sharpened by such an exercise is not to be sniffed at.

IT MIGHT HELP OTHERS TO UNDERSTAND

There is an overall cultural reason. Every generation has its own characteristics and has lived uniquely through a given span of years. In fact, generation is often more important than age. The two are often confused. What may be a 'generation' effect — your views on some social phenomenon such as long hair on teenagers or a dislike of modern pop music — is frequently interpreted as an 'old age' effect. This is a method of ensuring your generation is properly represented. It is a sort of social history. The sum of older people's reminiscence forms a popular portrait of their past and a significant chunk of the national story. Some historians have gone so far as to say that people born in the early part of the twentieth century have more to recall than most. Part way through your life arrived watersheds which, by any standards, were more portentous than many. Yours is the last generation which will have personally experienced life before the traumatic events of the Second World War, being the last of the pre-Pill, pre-atom bomb, pre-television, pre-pop, pre-everyday flying generation. It is something of a responsibility. Many older people give generously of their time to deliver the burden of their reminiscences to school-children in this matter of public interest, whilst some have their memoirs taped or written up in various collections, which, in future, will be part of the historical log of this passing period.

IT MIGHT BE PARTICULARLY VALUABLE TO YOUR FAMILY

This particular reason might have local application. One of the chief advantages in self-history is its value, sentimental as well as social, for your immediate family, with whom you might like to share, to whom you might like to bequeath, your sovereign memories. Your children and grandchildren might not always appreciate your anecdotes at the moment, especially if they tend to be rather long and rambling, but they will value them later. How often does one hear the bereaved relative, almost dazed by the disappearance of the source of all such knowledge, declaiming, *If only I'd got my father to write it all down . . . if only I'd taken my tape-recorder round to auntie's.* Too late, alas, too late — but not if you follow the instructions that are included in this little booklet.

IT MIGHT CHEER YOU UP

When all has been said and done, however, the main reason why you should embark on this autobiographical journey is for the hell of it, quite simply, because you will probably find it fascinating and because it will possibly fill you with lots of confidence. Moreover, it could be important to you philosophically, in the sense of putting your life in a sequence and in order, as you approach more nearly the end than the beginning of it. That is not defeatist talk: there is always something to plan for and look forward to in the future; that goes without saying. But there is a satisfaction to be gained in looking back and coming to terms with the events and happenings of your life. After all, as far as you are concerned, you are now the last generation. It may satisfy that thirst all of us, in some degree, encounter: the wish to seize on some sense of identity, and to place ourselves in the scheme of things. It may not be to everyone's taste: some may flee from the challenge or find it burdensome. Yet for the majority it can be beneficial, and research suggests that two-thirds of older people do find some advantage in reminiscence.

It is a question of what might be called Retrospect. For youth, there is a good deal of 'prospect'; in old age, there is the solace of 'retrospect'. You can look back, not in anger, but in tranquillity. It is vital to remember that we are all historical personages, passing through time. Never fall into the trap of thinking you have to be a Joseph Stalin or a Florence Nightingale before you enter the gallery of history. You are an historical character. You have the right and the privilege to regard yourself as such, and to embark on the one literary voyage that no one else is able to undertake — the sea trip through the tempests and doldrums of your own life. So, next time you are rabbiting on about the past and some upstart youngster complains and urges you to transfer to the present, be ready with the defiant answer: *Columbus-like, I have set sail in search of my true identity!*

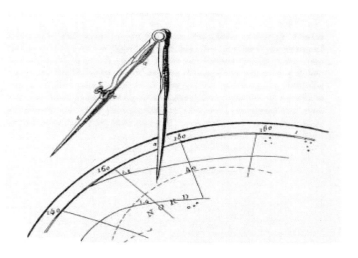

How should I chart the course?

It is all there. One's life, in its entirety, lies enormous enough behind us, just like the sea. We stand on the shore and marvel at its abundance. It is when we come to step into, or sail upon, the briny, that we need to sharpen our act, and learn a little about navigation. Eventually we can all remember a lot. The trouble is that we do not automatically remember it systematically. This is what probably puts off the younger generation when older people are telling their tales. If you wish to, follow a free association motif à la James Joyce, but it's not so rosy if you are trying to offer a tidy narrative to posterity in the shape of your grandchildren.

THE BROAD SWEEP

One approach is, of course, to scribble down everything you can recall over a period of time, and then reconstitute the material into some kind of more shapely product. The material becomes a sort of quarry, from which you take pieces and fashion them to your need. It is rather time-consuming, but it does suit some people, and that, to repeat, is the principal point of the exercise. Nonetheless, if you wish to create, either for your own use or for the use of others, a methodical pattern, then you will require some form of synopsis or agenda. Thus the following suggestions, irrespective of whether you begin with the synopsis, may be of value. In the event, many people seem to prefer the 'trigger' quality of a contents column of some kind: it both gets them going and at the same time provides them with a mould for their memories.

USEFUL TRIGGERS

Like the Pole Star on the olde-tyme voyage, certain events salient to every life are the most effective of guides. None is exclusive of the others: they should be utilised flexibly.

A. Culture-shocks

This is the term given to life-events of critical impact, of which the most dramatic — birth and death — are not ordinarily susceptible to the delights of self-history. Others are. They could become sub-heads of your self-history. Normally they relate to particular days, but don't be afraid to spread out over adjoining days or even weeks, if that is where the stimulus directs you:

My first day at school

My first birthday party

My first holiday and/or trip abroad

My first memory of a new baby brother or sister

My first memory of serious illness — my own

My first memory of serious illness, possibly death — a near relative, friend or neighbour, pet

My first change of school, eg, going to secondary school

My first love affair/date/romantic attachment/sexual encounter

My first memory of wartime disruption/first day in the services

My wedding day/honeymoon

My first day in a new house/flat

My first child

My first child — or subsequent children — facing similar culture-shocks, like teething, play-group, school, etc

My first job or move to a new job or promotion.

This should be sufficient to get you started. More children; more jobs; more homes; maybe even another husband or wife; these should follow naturally once you get the hang of the pegs upon which to hook your life events.

It may be that your life has been vividly exciting, with special features — a cliff-hanging war experience; a melodramatic divorce; a hazardous operation; emigration to Australia; a colourful career; and so forth. These, too, should begin to find their place in the narrative.

Don't follow the 'firsts' slavishly; omit some; include others; change the order to suit the narrative. Always remember: this is a guide, not a template.

B. Portmanteau memories

Especially in childhood (which is often the fulcrum of self-history and its most interesting aspect) memories are concertinaed. Christmas is a good example. Looking back, we recollect one Yuletide, rather than several, simply because, in many households, they took a similar form each year. That suggests another mould for your memories, along the lines of calendar themes.

A typical day when I was about three or four — if you are able, as some are, to remember that far back. Pre-school, that is

A typical day when I was about seven or eight — that is, when you were at elementary/primary school

A typical day when I was about thirteen — that is, when you had transferred, if you did, to a high/senior/grammar/secondary school

A typical day at work — this could be repeated at intervals to embrace a working life

The same for any other such aspects of everyday life.

My typical Christmas

My typical summer holiday

My typical week-end, Saturday and/or Sunday

My typical week at a given age — again, that is open to repetition at different ages

My typical year — tracing the characteristic year when you were, say, five to eleven, and/or during adolescence, and so on

My seasonal changes: several of the above 'days' are accessible to seasonal adjustment, allowing, for instance, for different leisure activities or entertainments or festivals in winter as opposed to summer.

C. Cameos

Your memories may be strongly influenced by particular people or places or, for instance, entertainments. You might find it revealing and stimulating to concentrate on profiles or descriptions of these. These might include:

Members of the extended family

Neighbours and local notables — the milkman, the policeman, etc. Friends and members of the gang

School teachers; superiors at work

As for locations, these would follow suit and are often best coped with in widening circles: my bedroom, my house, my garden, my street, my park or wood, my classroom, my school, my playground, my Sunday school, my church, my shops, my locale (village, district, etc), my town or nearest town, my countryside . . .

My wireless — and the programmes I enjoyed; my theatre/cinema — and the shows/films I enjoyed; my library — and the books/comics/ magazines I enjoyed.

D. Walking with history

You will probably find that memory is sharpened by your association with national and international events. This may become increasingly true as you examine the years as you grew older and, therefore, rather more aware of such happenings. Most people remember what they were doing, even as children, on, as Robb Wilton constantly reminded us, *the day war broke out*. Jack Kennedy's assassination and Princess Diana's fatal accident are other widely quoted examples — everybody remembers, it is said, what they were doing when they heard such epic news. Another advantage of this approach is that younger people enjoying your reverie will find the perspectives easier to grasp if they can place the material into a context of world and national events. You will have your own illustrations of this to spark you off, and some of them may be more localised events — the opening of a huge new factory; some local disaster or melodramatic incident. As an appendix, we have included a table of memorable twentieth century dates to assist you in your quest.

E. My diary
You may feel inclined to move straight ahead to a conventional framework, and perhaps the best way of doing that is to conceive the project as a remembered diary, either year by year, or social episode by social episode. It may be that others, having tried one or more of the triggers, and having collected an abundance of fruitful memories, may wish then to re-fashion the material into this more traditional pattern. You will have noticed that, just as all roads lead to Rome, all the stimuli, be they by year or incident or theme or whatever, eventually arrive at much the same data, which is eminently convertible to the sort of synopsis which might read:

My birth, my family and early years

My early schooling

My childhood and leisure activities

My later schooling

My adolescent social life

My first job

My working life (could be various episodes)

The War and I (could be various episodes)

My own home(s)

My adult social life

Romance and marriage (could be various episodes)

My children (ditto)

My travels at home and abroad

Changes at home and at work (various episodes)

My children grow up

My grandchildren arrive

My widow(er)hood

Obviously, this again is no more than a rough frame of reference. A year by year diary or log would be equally effective, and there might be all manner of 'episodes' to add to the above.

All in all, there are a number of standard triggers and structures which are workable, and which are all dependent on your self-vision, mood, temper and personality. What we hope is that one or several of those proposed here will lead you to construct your self-history, in part or whole.

All Shipshape and Bristol-Fashion

So much for plotting the course. How should you equip the ship and what stores will you need for the trip? In other words, what are the techniques for tidying up one's perhaps straggling memories and making them presentable in the form you have decided?

The page or the tape?
So far we have assumed that you will eventually write or type your memoirs. You might decide, however, to tape them. For the most part, the triggers discussed earlier apply to taping as well as writing. It may be assumed that this remains true for the following advice, although, to avoid undue awkwardness, we shall not constantly talk of writing and recording. One note to the tapers — you *may* want to plan your story on paper first, however primitively or roughly. Unless you have an exceptional talent for self-editing — or for editing lengthy miles of tape — it is unlikely you will get an authorised version from the raw fact of talking directly

into the recorder. Where the tape may also be useful is in interviewing surviving friends or relatives from way back who may remember you and who may be persuaded to reveal all. Possibly the ideal is something of each. the written version, plus, say, one tape describing a particular scene or incident, or maybe just saying simply why you have embarked on this *voyage of rediscovery*, as a complement or introduction to the written word. Your family will find pleasure in both, and it will be a solace for them always to have your voice to listen to — obviously a self-made video would be even better.

USING A TAPE RECORDER
First buy (or borrow) your tape recorder (unless you already have one) and familiarise yourself with how it works. For best sound quality get one with a socket for an external microphone as this gives much better quality than an internal microphone. A machine running off batteries gives a quieter recording. Experiment before you begin your real reminiscence or interviews — you can always tape over anything you don't want to keep. Try to record in a room away from traffic or other noise. The microphone should be 9" to 12" away from the person speaking.

THE BLANK PAGE
Never let this happen. There is nothing worse than that blockage of the blank sheet (or empty tape). Of course, the triggers described earlier are intended to get you firing on all cylinders, but even so . . . Do some thinking beforehand, especially right at the beginning of the project. Think about what you

are going to write when you are taking the dog for a walk or if you have been awakened early in the morning. Know approximately what you are going to write before you sit down with the wordless yardage of pad before you. Once you start it's not likely to be a problem — most people find that memories teem, jostling each other for attention. Above all, never stare at the blank page. Write something on it, even if it's only the name of the cat. You can cross it out later, but once you begin, however you begin, you are likely to be away and racing. Or, when you finish writing for the day, don't stop at a dead end — do try and leave yourself a verbal nudge for the next session.

THE LIMITATIONS

It is probably as well to have some idea, however vague, of what you wish to end with. Is it to be a slim volume of exquisite essentials, or is it to be twelve volumes of solid craftsmanship? It is important, when embarking on any product, including a piece of writing, to imagine how it is going to look in the end. If, for instance, you think you are going to write 100 pages, and you have planned 10 subsections, it is unwise to devote 90 pages to the first section. Without being too rigid, just ration yourself accordingly. Develop a sense of the structure you have decided upon for yourself.

Then there is time. You may decide to place a time-limit on yourself. You may say to yourself that you are prepared to spend six months or a year on this exercise. Give yourself a deadline. Next you might decide that you are going to spend every Wednesday morning on the project, or an hour every other evening, or whatever else is comfortable and yet efficient. In autobiography, as in the more fundamental matters of life itself, be regular.

At first, it may not be too easy, and it may be some time since you have put pen to paper in so formidable a way. There may be the equivalent of a pain-barrier, but stick at it, sustain your self-imposed timetable, and remember that many voyages are faced with dead calm in difficult passages. That also applies to the emotions. They may be disruptive at times. Self-history is not the act of those seeking bovine contentment. It is some kind of search for the truth, and sometimes it may be painful, uncomfortable or tearful to scratch away at some of the memory-traces. Part of the search for identity, that coming to terms with life and the past, may well balance unhappiness with pleasure. It is not escapism.

It may be a naive point, but, if you are writing by hand, write legibly, preferably on lined paper, and keep a decent margin. You will want to read it again in a year, and maybe amend or correct it. You may also want other people to read it.

SELF-CENSORSHIP
Other people reading it — now that raises a question or two. You must decide fairly early on whether you want your family, or anyone else for that matter, to have access to your self-history, or whether you are writing, 'dear diary' style, just to and for yourself. This is absolutely legitimate, and serves a valuable purpose. But if you are anxious for your family to enjoy with you, and after you, these reminiscences, and if you want them to be read as an account of your immediate ancestry and roots, then you may have to be

careful. There may be skeletons in your cupboard which you want to face yourself, as part of your journey towards that sense of personal identity and self-knowledge, which you feel would not be apposite for others to observe. So be it. There is no shame in that. It is your self-history, and your discretion is what matters most. Truth is multi-faceted. You must, in presentation, offer the face of truth with which you feel most at case.

SUPPORT SYSTEMS

You are advised to go into detail. It is the little nuances and flavours of memory which are often the most beguiling. When you embark, for instance, on the remembrance of a given day, such as the first day at a new school or the first day at work, begin at the beginning. Begin, that is, with waking up, and take it from there: tease out those minor, long-forgotten memories, like the clothes that you wore or the food you ate. It is that kind of detail that adds vitality to an essay in self-history. (You may decide not to write down all of these details but they may provide useful links in a chain of memories.)

There may be other triggers which you might, so to speak, turn on yourself. There may be the potency of music — some dance band tune which, as popular music so often can, brings memory flooding back. There are smells to be remembered and perhaps re-found for stimulus. The memory of certain foods, even unpleasant ones, may have remained with you and be related to particular moments in your life. Photographs are an obvious source. There may be other memorabilia — letters and postcards, old documents like birth certificates or old gas bills, old newspapers, old objects. When these have served their purpose as sources, you may then utilise them as resources, and possibly include them in your collection. You may even want to create a *Lifescape* *.

Don't forget, if you are doing any taping, to include some of that poignant music for good measure. And don't be afraid of creative writing. Some self-histories gain where the writer has decided to represent some incident in the form of a short story or some close relationship in the form of a poem. (Your memoirs need not always take the same form — a story, poem or dialogue may be inter-leafed with a more straight-forward recounting.)

These kinds of supports are extremely useful. As for the writing itself, it is best to keep it simple, presenting your account in clear-cut, normally short sentences. Keep a dictionary handy, just to check on the occasional spelling, especially where the results are to be read by others. As for punctuation, the safety test is to read what you have written aloud. Punctuation is mainly breathing on paper — one pause for a comma; three for a full stop. If it makes sense orally, using your punctuation for pausing, then it should make sense when written down.

One of the best support systems is to find a companion — your spouse; a friend; a neighbour — who is also interested in such a project. Better still, you may find a group of remi-niscence 'freaks'. Some University of the Third Age (U3A) groups, for instance, organise such activities. Most libraries will be able to give you details of local history or oral history societies. There is no doubt that other people's enthusiasm and ideas can be invigorating, and one often finds an explosion of memories as a consequence. One such group of about 20 old people were prompted with 'a typical day when they were about seven years old', the aim being to work through the entire day, including the hours at school, over an afternoon session. Two and a half hours passed and the group had not left their collective houses: they were still recalling getting up on a cold morning and putting bare feet on chilly linoleum, eating Force for breakfast and contemplating Sunny Jim . . . That said, it is not everybody's choice to work in tandem or in a group. Some may prefer the solitary approach.

There may be outside forms of support by way of books or slides. Age Exchange, for instance, has produced various packs and manuals to assist in the fascinating business of reminiscence. In the end, however, you will find yourself, with pen poised and brow furrowed, the sole arbiter of your autobiography, the veritable captain of your fate on this *voyage of rediscovery*.

---

* a *Lifescape* is a collage of memorabilia. See page 36 for details.

Landfall

Eventually it is done. It is worth sparing a moment to congratulate yourself and to cogitate on what you have achieved. Consider the true status of memory. Self-history is different from history as such, in so far as it mainly relies on your memory alone, whereas in the ordinary course of history you would expect some evidence and cross-referencing to back-up your assertions. For many facts you will be able to do this — the birth certificate or marriage lines, for example. But, generally you are committing your memories to paper. This means that they are subjective and subject to the distortions of time, while, in some cases, you may not be able to distinguish concisely between what you remember and what you were told so often that it became a memory. As long as this is recognised as such, there is no problem. Self-history has its own validity, and that rests on the authenticity of each person's memory as his/her own personal intellectual powerhouse.

It is a well-known fact that memories are made up of what you remember and not what happened. Simulated experiments, in which people have all viewed a recorded incident and then reported what they saw right away and then at regular intervals, have demonstrated this. There is a genuine correlation between the continued reports and the first report, that is, the initial memorisation; and much less with the actual events. In short, you remember, not what happened, but what you first remembered as having happened. If, for sixty years, you have recollected your grandfather as hatless at a graveside, it is very difficult to amend a memory so that he is wearing a hat, supposing that he was.

So the emphasis in self-history is on the self. What you are sharing, first with yourself, and next, if they are lucky, with your family, and maybe others, is the real self as revealed by and interpreted by your memories. To be honest, this means it does not differ much from most autobiographies of famous people, however they might protest that they revealed themselves, as Cromwell said, 'warts and all'. Cromwell said that as he instructed his portrait painter, for he was shrewdly aware that portraits are open, for good or ill, to prejudice. Perhaps one way of describing self-history is to see it as a form of self-portrait, acknowledging that it is your 'self' that you are revealing, and not necessarily some strictly objective photographic-like image.

A TWENTIETH CENTURY ALMANAC

Instead of sea-charts for the journey, it was felt that some kind of chronological chronometer might be of use, a log of those stirring events which you might consider as an aide-memoir to help you plot your course, or perhaps a star chart against which you plot your own particular comet!

1901 Death of Queen Victoria
     Theodore Roosevelt became President of the USA
     Marconi received first transatlantic 'bending' radio
     signal (round the curve of the earth)
1906 Liberals win general election
1908 Old Age Pensions introduced
     Hoover Suction Sweeping Company produced first
     'hoover'
1910 Death of Edward VII
     Death of Florence Nightingale
1911 Marie Curie, discoverer of radium (1898), became
     first person to win two Nobel Prizes and first woman
     Nobelist
     Amundsen reaches the South Pole
1912 Sinking of the Titanic
1913 Women's skirts go above the ankle
1914 First World War breaks out
1916 Captain Leefe Robinson won the first VC over
     England shooting down Zeppelin L21, airship
     bomber
     Battle of the Somme

1917 Start of Russian Revolution
1918 Big Bertha large calibre gun shelled Paris
     End of the First World War
     Women over 30 get the vote in Britain
1919 Great Flu Epidemic
1920 Civil War in Ireland
     League of Nations' first meeting
1922 Tomb of Tutankhamen discovered by Howard Carter
1923 First broadcast of Big Ben chimes
1924 First Labour government
     Death of Lenin
     Malcolm Campbell sets land speed record in
     Bluebird
1925 Metro Goldwyn Mayer film studio established
1926 General Strike
1927 First major sound film — *The Jazz Singer*
1928 Maginot Line fortifications begun
1931 Death of Dame Nellie Melba
1932 May West's film debut
1933 Hitler comes to power
1936 Abdication of Edward VIII
     Spanish Civil War
     Fred Perry wins Wimbledon for the third time
1937 Belisha Beacon first used
     Snow White is first feature-length cartoon film
1938 Chamberlain at Munich
1939 Outbreak of Second World War
     Film *Gone With the Wind*
1940 Churchill becomes premier
     Dunkirk
1941 Death of Fred Karno, he of the famous 'army'

1945 End of War
　　Attlee becomes Labour prime minister
　　Atom bombs dropped on Hiroshima and Nagasaki
1946 United Nations replaces League of Nations
1947 Indian independence and the creation of Pakistan
1948 Olympics held at London's White City
1950 Korean War begins
　　McCarthy 'red' witch-hunt
1951 Festival of Britain
1952 Teddy Boy cult of pseudo-Edwardian dress
1953 Coronation of Elizabeth II
　　Conquest of Everest
　　Death of Stalin
1956 Suez crisis
　　Russian invasion of Hungary
1958 Charles de Gaulle returns as President of France
1959 Macmillan wins 'never had it so good' election
1961 Yuri Gagarin is first man in space
1963 President Kennedy assassinated
　　Exposure of Rachmanism — exploitation of tenants
　　The Beatles
1965 The Mini skirt
1966 England win World Cup at football
1967 Devaluation of the pound
1968 Northern Ireland troubles flare up
　　Student riots in USA and France
1969 Americans put first man on the moon
1970 Edward Heath becomes premier
1974 National miners' strike
　　Three-day week
1975 Common Market referendum

1979 Margaret Thatcher comes to power
1982 Falklands War
1984 Miners' strike
1986 Channel Tunnel agreed
1991 End of Cold War with realignment of Eastern Europe
1992 Bill Clinton elected President of USA
1994 Nelson Mandela elected President of South Africa
      National Lottery introduced
1997 Tony Blair became Prime Minister in UK
      Death of Princess Diana
      Dolly the sheep cloned
1998 'Good Friday' agreement in Northern Ireland
2000 Human 'Genome' pattern completed

Useful Addresses

Age Exchange Reminiscence Centre, 11 Blackheath Village, London SE3 9LA. Tel: 020 8318 9105.
Website: www.age-exchange.org.uk.
Has an extensive list of publications and reminiscence resources. A hands-on reminiscence museum. Reminiscence training courses.

National Life Story Collection, British Library National Sound Archive, 96 Euston Road, London NW1 2DB.
Tel: 020 7412 7404.
Publications and advice on recording life stories.

Oral History Society (as for National Life Story Collection above)

University of the Third Age (U3A), 19 East Street, Bromley BR1 1QH.   Tel: 020 8466 6139
Website: www.u3a.org.uk. Send an SAE for contact details of your nearest U3A. Many U3As have study groups on local and personal history.

Your library will have information on **local history societies.**

OTHER BOOKS BY ERIC MIDWINTER IN THE
LIFELINES SERIES
**Available — postfree — from Third Age Press,
6 Parkside Gardens, London SW19 5EY**
Encore: a guide to planning a celebration of your life
An unusual and useful booklet that encourages you to think about
the ways you would like to be remembered, hopefully in the
distant future. 1993   20 pp   ISBN 1 898576 02 5   £2.00

*The Rhubarb People: Eric Midwinter's 'Voyage of
Rediscovery'* , set in Manchester in the 1930s . . . is
published as a booklet but also as a 90-minute audio
cassette read by the author. The cassette includes useful tips on
writing or recording your story. 1993 32pages ISBN   1
898576 01 7   Booklet: £4.00.   Audio cassette £5.00

Getting To Know Me . . . is aimed at carers and families of
people in care. It provides the opportunity to create a profile of
an older person ~ their background and relationships, likes and
dislikes, as well as record the practical information needed to
make the caring process a positive experience for all concerned.
1996   24pages   ISBN 1 898576 07 6   £2.00

---

* *Lifescapes: the landscapes of a lifetime* by Enid Irving
. . . introduces a whole new art form . . . a *'Lifescape'* is a
collage of memories. Make one just for fun or as a very special
family heirloom. *Lifescapes* can be made by individuals,in
groups, as a family or as an intergenerational activity. The result-
ing *Lifescape* is not only decorative but serves to increase
understanding of the whole person and stimulate memory.1996
24pages   ISBN 1 898576 08 4   £4.00